# Contents

## 1 Introduction: who should read this manual?

There are numerous "generic" job search books that are supposed to help regardless of what sector of the job market you target. Quantitative Finance and Financial Engineering jobs are also covered in a few sources. These manuals focus mainly on mastering the quantitative part of the job interview. "Behavioral", or "soft" questions are usually glossed over. The biggest problem is that the available advice on how to get interviews in the first place is insufficient and lacking in specificity.

This void is especially painful for the job seekers who are "disadvantaged" in one way or another. For instance, to boost your resume, it is suggested that you get a summer internship while in school. This sounds reasonable enough – until you find out that major financial institutions hire their interns through on-campus visits, and their visit list does not include your university. There are other ways in which you can be disadvantaged, making many available job search tips sound like a nasty joke. The following list summarizes the possible complications you may have to deal with:

(A) You are an entry-level candidate (less than 2 years of experience *after* graduation);

(B) You require a work permit to work in this country (e.g., you are not a U.S. resident / green card holder);

(C) The financial job market is in recession (2001-2003, 2008-?);

(D) Your school is not considered top-tier in the quant finance community;

(E) The connections between your school and quant industry are weak (e.g., major banks do not visit your campus);

(F) Your communication / interviewing skills are not that good;

(G) You live / study far away from major financial centers (London, New York, etc).

If you don't fit this list (e.g., you are a U.S. citizen graduating with a PhD from Princeton into a booming job market), this manual is not for you. You can get along with the job search literature that is already available. If, on the other hand, your situation is a good fit to the list above, this manual will help you out. After all, it's been written by a person who fitted the entire list from (A) to (G) and still managed to succeed.

## 2 What to expect from this book

 I amafraid some advice I give in this manual (Section 8) might make me non-hireable in the future.

The important thing is, as I mentioned in Introduction, I was (and still am) a "perfectly" disadvantaged job candidate, fitting all of the items in the list from (A) to (G). Despite that, I managed to find two quant internships while at university and a long-term quant position right upon graduation. Unfortunately, I didn't keep it for too long, and, as of October 2010, I am in the middle of another job search. This manual is based on my personal experience gathered while I looked for internships and permanent positions between 2005 and 2010. All of it took place in the U.S., but most of this manual applies to other countries as well.

I would like to emphasize that the advice I give here is designed specifically for disadvantaged job candidates, denoted "DC" everywhere below. If I say something like "don't bother to do X" or "if you do Y, the chance of success is 50%", all this is *conditional* on your being a DC. If you are not exactly a DC, adjust my recommendations for your specific situation as you see fit. Also, I assume that you are going to graduate with at least a Master's degree in a quantitative discipline, and that the position you target requires at least that level of education.

As I mentioned in Introduction, almost all of the current quant guides do not pay enough attention to the job search process itself and the "soft" phase of interviewing. The only exception is the book of Jiu (2010). To a certain degree, my manual is a result of taking the "strategic" advice of Jiu and making it more "tactical" and suitable for the needs of a DC. I highly recommend you get the revised 2010 paperback edition of Jiu's book. Its content pertaining to the job hunting and interviewing has not changed since the 2007 edition, but it is still very helpful.

I would like to express my gratitude to Marina Byezhanova, a personal friend of mine. She helped me find and polish the answers to concrete "soft" interview questions in Section 8. Marina's advice is derived from her own long and successful work as a headhunter in Montreal, Canada. Although my general attitude towards headhunters is far from positive, Marina is a rare exception. It is too bad that my own job search has always been limited to the

U.S. boundaries.

A few technical notes: some information in this manual is time-sensitive, and I tried to make it accurate as of October-November 2010. This also includes Web links, and, in case they break, I provide keywords that you can use to find the corresponding content via Google. The capital letters (A) – (G) in the text below will always refer to the list in Introduction. The word "bank" refers to any firm that might have quant finance openings.

Sections 3-7 describe how to organize and perform a successful job search. Section 8 is aimed at helping you with the interviewing process, with a special emphasis on "behavioral", or "soft" interview questions. Finally, from Section 9 you will learn how to boost your resume by becoming a certified C++ developer.

**3 Thinking like a quant: what NOT to do and why**

Quantitative trading is a secretive line of business: employees are often bound by non-disclosure and non-compete agreements. A layman would say that it's necessary to protect profitable trading techniques. That makes sense, but, as a quant, you must recognize that concealing the strategies that are *unprofitable* is just as important. Suppose your quant trading firm has invested $500,000 (cost of wages, equipment, time) in a new trading idea that turned out to be a dead end. You suspect that your competitor is about to try a very similar strategy. Would you give him a friendly warning that he is about to waste half a million dollars? Probably not.

On the other hand, your competitor could be very grateful to a consultant who would save him half a million. Think of it: the consultant could earn a handsome fee (say, 10%, or $50,000) just by advising on what NOT to do. The same reasoning applies to job search. If you know which strategies do NOT work, you can gain an edge by focusing your attention elsewhere. Let me review some popular job search tips that are NOT effective for a DC, and explain why I consider them pretty useless.

**Tip 1.** *Use the company website to apply for a posted job / internship opening.*

*Reality:* a large percentage of job openings does not become publicly available at all. Suppose you are Head of Quantitative Research at XYZ bank who needs to hire a new team member. Why should you post the opening and have strangers apply? Most likely, the position will be filled by someone you know or someone who is recommended by someone you know. That's why, even when you see a posted opening, there is a good chance that it doesn't really exist: it is known in advance that the position will be filled by an "internal" candidate. In that case, the job is posted publicly just for "compliance" or other legal reasons. Besides, the application processing software is often faulty and your CV could be lost and/or will never be read by a human being.

Finally, you have to consider your competition. If you apply online for a position with a bigger name like Goldman Sachs, how many people do you think will do exactly the same? I'd say 100 at least, and many of them have CVs a lot stronger than yours (remember that you are a DC).

The same is true for internships with big banks: when online applications are available, every quant student in the US sees them and you have to beat a fierce competition to get in. In addition, major banks tend to hire interns via on-campus visits, and an online ad is just the first step in that process. If your campus is not on the visit list, you are locked out. Also, such applications are fairly time-consuming because one has to create a detailed profile over and over again.

The good news is that, for both internships and permanent positions, there is a "hidden" job market. This manual will show you how to find and tap it.

**Tip 2.** *Ask your professors for help in your job search.*

*Reality:* if item (E) from Introduction rings true for you, this tip is useless. In my university, the professors were great as teachers and researchers, but couldn't care less about the industrial careers of the graduates. It is understandable, because marketing someone to the industry is not a professor's job.

To take this issue further, two-year Financial Engineering type programs are frequently said to be too expensive for the quality of education they provide. At the same time, they often strive to market their graduates to the industrial sector. If this results in plum internships and jobs for the students and graduates, the seemingly high tuition may be worth it after all.

**Tip 3.** *Attend job fairs.*

*Reality:* the problem is similar to that of Tip 2. In my case, the job fairs on campus were plenty, but the numerous employers presented there had little to do with the quant sector. In fact, such banks as J.P. Morgan and Morgan Stanley did visit our campus, but it was to hire for the IT, Operations, and similar non-quant divisions. As for off-campus quant job fairs, they are still very few and far between (Section 5.3).

**Tip 4.** *Your university must have something like a Student Career Center that should help.*

*Reality:* I am sure that my university's Student Career Center is a great thing, but not when it comes to finding a quant position. First of all, the bulk of its activity was focused on placing college graduates, not M.S. and Ph.D. people. Secondly, there is item (E) again: if your university is not visited by quant employers in one way or another, the Student Career Center is not helpful when it comes to quant jobs and internships.

**Tip 5.** *Attend professional networking events.*

*Reality:* it's actually a useful thing, but not in the sense that it will directly result in a job offer from someone you met there. First of all, the majority of attendees are likely to be the same quant wannabes as you.

Second, as a DC, you must compile a massive job search database, and there are only so many hands you can shake. Finally, if item (G) rings a bell for you, it may be unproductive to spend $400-$800 on a trip to NYC or wherever the event takes place. As this manual will show you, there are better ways to invest money in your job search.

**Tip 6.** *Use headhunters.*

By "headhunter", I mean an individual or firm who is not employed by, say, Goldman Sachs, but who claim they can get you hired if they take your CV and submit it to Goldman. If you are hired, Goldman (not you) will pay the headhunter. Headhunters can also call themselves "recruiters", which is confusing because a "corporate recruiter" is a person who is employed by the Human Resources department of Goldman on a permanent basis.

*Reality:* for a DC, headhunters are virtually useless. The current level of professionalism in quant finance headhunting is worse than anywhere else in the U.S. economy. Of course, I am not familiar with the entire U.S. economy. I just can't see how it can be any worse than what I saw in the quant sector.

If you come across a website of a headhunting ("recruiting") firm and see some attractive quant jobs posted, you may safely assume that all of them are fakes. All such firms want is to get your CV and, in the best case, do nothing with it. The worst case is when your CV is submitted for the same job by more than one headhunter without your knowledge. In that case, your candidacy can be dropped altogether, because the employer does not wish to sort out which headhunter is to get the finder's fee.

Another thing these "recruiting professionals" can do is to call you and say that, in order to "help" you, you should first tell them all about the applications you have made. As soon as they know where you have applied and with whom you talked, they submit a bunch of their own candidates for the very same position(s), creating extra competition for you. I will talk more about headhunters below, but I hope you caught my drift by now.

If you decide to commit much of your hope and/or resources to a particular job search avenue, it would be great to have some hard evidence that it works not only "in general" but also for a DC like yourself. Try to gain that information. For instance, has anybody in your class heard of a single person who got a quant position through your Student Career Center? Can any of your associates name a quant headhunter who is good not only at talking? Is your classmate sure that her expensive trip to a networking event in New York paid off? (her picking up that cute guy in a Midtown bar is not going to count).

If you have no information and still need to make a decision, you'll be better off eliminating options that match the "black list" above. I am sure that after you finish reading this manual, you'll be able to develop some ideas of your own. They may or may not work, but as long as they are not in the "black list", they are worth trying.

# 4 Building the core of your own job search machine

## 4.1 Time for a bold, unstoppable plan: your overall strategy

I have some unpleasant news for you: being a DC implies that your job search strategy should be drastically different from that of an "advantaged" candidate – just like your background is different from his/hers. To level your chances with those of an "advantaged" person, the amount of time and effort to invest in your job search should be at least 20 times greater. For instance, it may take an "advantaged" person 5-10 applications to obtain a plum quant internship at a bank; you, on the other hand, must submit at least 250 applications.

The most effective way to land a position is to leverage personal connections. This doesn't imply that you should have lots of "real" friends working in the quant industry. All it means is that you should be able to get in touch with such people via email and have them read your CV. All other job search methods are subordinate to this core strategy: it makes sense to invest in them only if you have spare time / money you can't invest in increasing the number of reachable individuals.

Before you start building your job search database, I strongly suggest that you think of "plan B", i.e. figure out what kind of work you can do outside the world of quant finance. After that, build your network accordingly. This is especially relevant for DCs who are not U.S. residents and who will be forced to leave the U.S. boundaries unless employed. Also, your geographical restrictions may reduce your chances drastically. It's enough to say that, in USA, over 90% of hedge fund assets are concentrated in the New England area, and about 1/3 of *global* hedge fund assets are managed from Connecticut alone. Importantly, once you start looking outside the quant finance sector, some of the "negative" advice I gave in Section 3 can become invalid. For instance, you may find that your professors do have useful ties with the industry, some headhunters are actually helpful, etc.

In Sections 4.2-6, I am going to describe in detail how to build a list of individual connections and what to expect from some "conventional" job search tools. In Section 7, I outline a comprehensive job search plan where several strategies are combined.

## 4.2 LinkedIn: a game of very large numbers

LinkedIn ([www.linkedin.com](http://www.linkedin.com)) is a worldwide online professional network. It provides access to millions of people's professional profiles and it is the backbone of my own job search machine. While looking for long-term positions in 2008-2010, I invested over $1000 in LinkedIn, and I think it was worth it: upon graduation, I obtained a permanent position thanks to LinkedIn. My internship search took place before I got a LinkedIn profile. Still, it was based on reaching out to a large number of people, and this is also the main idea behind LinkedIn. I wish I were paid for advertising this network here, but, believe me, I am not. Also, my expenses could have been cut by at least 25% if I had known in advance a few tricks I will share below.

Each LinkedIn profile looks (or, at least, is supposed to look) like an electronic resume, supplied with a small optional photo (typically, a headshot). One can also post PowerPoint presentations, PDF and Word files, book reviews, and more. New features are added continuously, and changes in the interface are introduced every now and then. There's a separate niche in the book market occupied by manuals on "how to use LinkedIn". I started with a book of that kind, but I am not recommending it here because by now it has become obsolete. I will talk about the main things you should know below, but I still suggest you purchase an up-to-date LinkedIn book.

## 4.3 Seizing the beachhead: your profile and connections

First of all, you have to register (it's free) and complete your LinkedIn profile. I would recommend that you start with your resume first and then turn it into a profile. I find the books of Yate (2010) and Jiu (2010) quite helpful for the composition of resumes, CVs, and cover letters. The profile is basically an expanded resume where you use 3-4 pages instead of a resume's limit of 1-2. While placing a photo in a resume is a big no, I find it very useful on LinkedIn. Its main purpose is identification, because some people have similar names, and you will never meet the majority of your connections in person. Keep in mind that your profile is going to be searched by keywords, and including them explicitly is a good idea. The profile should be as complete and appealing as possible before you start sending invitations to strangers.

A standard part of your LinkedIn profile is a link to your website, and I recommend you create one. Although you can post files on LinkedIn, it's not nearly as flexible and representative as your own website can be. When you are new to the quant field and don't have much to share, a natural question is what to post. Even in that case, you can post anything that goes to show you are serious about getting into the field: your resume (don't make it downloadable because you want to control where it goes), relevant projects you completed at school, quant papers you find interesting, and so on. Avoid posting anything personal, including photos (your headshot is already available on LinkedIn, and that's enough). Another advantage of the website is that you can place your resume in an online folder and then send out a hyperlink to it. That way, you can modify the underlying file and the link you shared months ago will still point to an up-to-date resume. Most likely, having a website won't help you when competing against "advantaged" job-seekers. Still, you will certainly look preferable against the background of other DCs.

LinkedIn distinguishes between 3 types of connections:

1) $1^{st}$ degree connections. You acquire them by sending a so-called Invitation to an individual who later accepts it by clicking the corresponding button. Likewise, you can receive an Invitation from someone else and accept it. After that, two things happen:

a) You can exchange LinkedIn messages for free. At this point, a LinkedIn message is a simple text message that doesn't allow attachments. If you want to share a file, you can share a hyperlink to it.

b) You new connection is added to the list of your $1^{st}$ degree connections. As of 11/2010, this list can be found by clicking on "Contacts" and then "My Connections". Click on any $1^{st}$ degree profile and you will see the person's email address, so a conventional email exchange is also available.

The list can be made "open" by ticking the corresponding option in the Settings page. This simply means your $1^{st}$ degree connections can see the entire list of yours. In general, I recommend being as "open" in your settings as possible.


2) $2^{nd}$ degree connections. A $2^{nd}$ degree person is connected to one of your $1^{st}$ degree connections, but not to you. Unlike with $1^{st}$ degree connections, here you can't exchange LinkedIn messages for free.

3) $3^{rd}$ degree connections. A $3^{rd}$ degree person is connected to you only

through one of your 2<sup>nd</sup> degree connections. Typically, you can't exchange free LinkedIn messages with a 3<sup>rd</sup> degree person, and their names look like "Jane K." to you. You can't see the full name unless you are a paid member. If a person is more than 3 degrees away from you, he/she is considered "outside your network". Even the first name of such person is often invisible to you.

As an example, a profile may have 300 of 1<sup>st</sup> degree connections, 100,000 of  2<sup>nd</sup> degree connections, and 3 million of 3<sup>rd</sup> degree connections. Now you can see why LinkedIn plays the core part in my job search. This would have been unthinkable some 8 years ago when LinkedIn was just founded.

### 4.4 How many would attend your funeral? Starting your network

As of 11/2010, you can send an Invitation to the following groups of people:

1) Colleagues. This implies that your profiles should indicate that both of you work (worked) for the same company.

2) Business partners. Similar to 1).

3) Classmates. Same as above, only it's an educational institution instead of a company.

4) Group members. You should belong to the same LinkedIn group.

5) Friends. This is used for your personal friends.

6) Other. This option can be used only if you know the recipient's email address.

After you set up your account, you can invite anyone simply by claiming that he / she is your friend. The important thing to remember is that the recipient of your Invitation can push a button "I don't know this person", which amounts to a complaint. If a certain number of complaints builds up, your account will be suspended. After that, you can unfreeze it, but, from that moment on, you will be required to provide the recipient's email address even when you use Friend option. If you specify the recipient's email address in the invitation, he won't be able to complain even when he can't recall who you are.

Correspondingly, your first few steps should consist in utilizing the options 1) – 6) above safely, i.e. inviting the people whose email address you know (via "Other"), and/or the people who remember you well. You can import an address book from your email client (e.g., Microsoft Outlook) or enter emails manually, and invitations will be sent to the corresponding LinkedIn members. This will work if there's a match between your input and the email address the recipient used to set up his/her account. It's a good idea to make your Invitation personalized instead of using the standard one.

I would start with inviting the students who attend the same Quantitative Finance program as yourself. Those who will graduate sooner than you should be your primary target group because they are more likely to be helpful with respect to both internship and permanent job search. Connecting to your current or junior classmates also makes sense as a long-term investment: in the future, you may find yourself in a position when you are unemployed and they are not.

## 4.5 And I will make you fishers of men: extending your network

The next step would be to join as many relevant LinkedIn groups as you can (check out the "Groups" tab). The advantages of that are as follows:

1) An increase in overall visibility of your profile.

2) You can often exchange free messages with the group members, regardless of how many links separates you.

3) You can send invitations to other group members without using the questionable Friend option. It is definitely better than to claim to be someone's friend when, in fact, you are not.

The total number of groups you can join is limited to 50, and it's fairly easy to find about 50 groups that have to do with Quantitative Finance, Financial Engineering, or "generic" quantitative modeling. The admission criteria are not strict, because each group wants to be large.

Next, you should identify more LinkedIn members whom you would like to see in your network. I would rank one's potential connections in the order of importance as follows:

1) Individuals whose educational background is similar to yours and who already occupy a position that seems appealing to you. In other words, any person whom you see as a future boss or co-worker.

2) HR managers employed by the companies that are known to hire quants.

3) Any individual who may be connected directly to 1) or 2), including headhunters. Remember that, typically, you can send free LinkedIn messages to your $2^{nd}$ degree connections.

Thanks to a large number of available "Advanced Search" options, finding such people is easy. You can use the following search criteria:

1) Keywords, with Boolean logic: AND, OR, NOT, possibly with parentheses

2) First and Last Name

3) Location

4) Job title

5) Company

6) School

7) Industry

8) A few other options

For instance, I would like to find PhD – level quants in Los Angeles, my search options can be set as:

1) Quantitative AND PhD

2)

3) Zipcode 90012 within 75 miles

4)

5)

6)

7) Financial Services

Since L.A. is not a quant city, this search returns only 14 hits. Try this in NYC area and see the difference.

The next question is how exactly to invite these strangers into your network. Technically, an Invitation is a favored choice because the recipient only has to push the "Accept" button. To increase the proportion of people whom you can invite via the "Other" option, I recommend using LinkedIn combined with Jigsaw.com (www.jigsaw.com). In short, Jigsaw is a huge database of people's business cards searchable by name, position title, company name, geographical location, etc.

Under the basic plan (the most expensive on average), the cost of obtaining someone's email is $5, which is not as pricey as it seems. First of all, you can get an instant refund just by claiming that the business card you purchased is stale or has become stale. All you have to do is to click a couple of buttons. However, this option is not to be abused because whoever supplied the information can contest your claim. Secondly, you can earn credits if you supply your own contacts to Jigsaw, e.g. by using the business cards you collected at a networking event. Also, I noticed that the "Faculty" page of almost all US universities contains contact information for the employed professors. This can be used for adding new entries to Jigsaw to save your money.

Another useful application is Xobni ("inbox" reversed), an add-on to the email client (I use the free version). Given an email address, Xobni checks automatically whether there is a corresponding profile on LinkedIn, Facebook, or Twitter. If a profile is found, it provides a link to it.

Your overall objective is to send out as many Invitations as you can. Try to reduce the chances that your recipient complains about getting an Invitation from a stranger. For instance, if you went to the same school or belong to the same LinkedIn group, invite via the "Classmate" or "Group" option as opposed to the "Friend". If and when all other options are exhausted, I do recommend you take the "Friend" route. Since one's network grows exponentially, the extra contacts you can get via "Friend" today will result in a significantly larger network in a few months' time.

## 4.6 A cry from afar: Introductions and Inmails

If sending an Invitation the way described above is not an option, you can recourse to sending a message to ask if the recipient wants to join. That means you have to provide your email address so that the recipient use it to invite you, or ask for his/her email address to invite him/her yourself. Note that the cumulative number of Invitations one can send over an account's lifetime is limited to 3000, so some people may want to limit the number of outgoing Invitations. The considerable flaw of sending a message is that it requires the recipient to do a lot more than a single click to join your network.

The following types of LinkedIn members are likely to be reachable:

1) People in the same LinkedIn group.

2) $2^{nd}$ and $3^{rd}$ degree connections can be reached via Introduction.

3) Almost any LinkedIn member can be reached via Inmail (it's not free).

4) An email address can be specified in one's profile. Not all people try to conceal it.

5) You can use "LinkedIn Questions and Answers" feature to answer someone's question. Also, you can reply to someone who replied to the question you posted in that section. In either case, you effectively exchange free messages.

LinkedIn Introductions can be illustrated as follows: suppose John is your $1^{st}$ degree connection. He is connected to Mary (your $2^{nd}$ degree connection), and Mary is connected to Robert (your $3^{rd}$ degree connection). If you want to send a message to Robert, you first direct it to John. If John is nice enough, he will direct it to Mary. If Mary is nice enough, she will direct it to Robert. This feature is not reliable because your message tends to get stuck somewhere in the middle. Also, when Robert clicks the button "Accept Introduction", it does NOT mean that Robert becomes your $1^{st}$ degree connection, and most LinkedIn members do not realize that. Introductions are slow and confusing, but, still, they offer a chance to expand one's network for free.

An Inmail allows you to send one message to almost any LinkedIn member. If she doesn't reply within 7 days, you get your credit back on day 8. Correspondingly, your message must mention explicitly that, if the recipient is not interested, she should not reply. That way, you can recycle your Inmail credits a large number of times (for 90 days at least) and cut your costs drastically. The worst way to acquire Inmails is to buy them outside a subscription plan, which amounts to $10 per Inmail. At this point, the most cost efficient plan is "Executive", where you pay $100 and get 25 Inmails a month.

Below I give a few approximate samples of what you should tell people to lure them into your network. However, the quality of your LinkedIn profile is still a decisive factor here.

*LinkedIn Invitation sent to a stranger via the "Friend" option:*

Dear Dr. Zhang:

Even though we haven't met, I felt compelled to use the Friend option to send you an invitation. Your LinkedIn profile is very impressive. As a future fellow quant, I would be honored to have you in my network. Please accept my invitation.

Sincerely,


*LinkedIn message (a free one):*

Dear Ms. Jennings:

As somebody new to LinkedIn, I am reaching out to fellow quantitative professionals, and I noticed your impressive profile. Although I am still a student, I am passionate about Quant Finance and would like to join the industry after graduation. Please, consider joining my network. You can send me an invitation via abc@gmail.com. Alternatively, you could let me have your email address so that I invite you.

Regards,
name

*LinkedIn Introduction:*

Dear Mr. Robinson:

I am attempting to extend the network of my fellow quantitative professionals, and I noticed your impressive profile. Although I am still a student, I am passionate about Quant Finance and would like to join the industry after graduation. Please, consider joining my network.

Note that if you just click the "Accept Introduction" button, we are not going to connect. To get connected, you will need to send me an invitation via abc@gmail.com or let me have your email address so that I could invite you.

Regards,
abc

*LinkedIn Inmail:*

Dear Matthew:

I am sorry I couldn't use your full name because I can only see your first name.

Being new to LinkedIn, I am reaching out to fellow quantitative professionals, and your profile attracted me because I liked your recent paper "Efficient Monte-Carlo Pricing of IR exotics". Please, consider joining my network. You can send me an invitation via abc@gmail.com or let me have your email address so that I could invite you.If you are not interested in connecting, please do NOT reply to this Inmail.

Yours sincerely,

name

It is not very polite to address a stranger by his/her first name, and that's exactly why LinkedIn tries to make extra money on hiding the last name of your $3^{rd}$ degree connections. The explicit "do NOT reply" is important here. You don't want to get a polite "Sorry, I only connect with someone I know" that wastes between \$4 and \$10 of your Inmail investment. It's enough that 5-10% of the people will send you useless replies despite "do NOT reply" request.

Keeping track of your interactions with people is crucial in order to avoid confusion and duplication. I create an Excel table and keep track of all contacts I made. For each individual, I record his/her name, company, location, and when and how he/she was contacted. When I was just starting to explore the U.S. job market, I had a similar table for companies because I applied through corporate websites a lot, but now I have less use for it thanks to my larger network.

Building a decent (over 150 contacts) network takes at least 6 months. The sooner you start, the cheaper your job search will be, and the better your chance for success. If you haven't managed to build a large network, investing massively in Inmails and Jigsaw during the active phase of job search (Section 7) might be a way out, although I have not tried it myself.

# 5 Conventional job search tools: a second glance

## 5.1 Companies: big fish and small fry

For a newbie job-seeker, it is natural to think of a prospective employer as a certain company, e.g., Goldman Sachs, Morgan Stanley, etc. However, as my network of individuals grew, I found less and less reasons to contact companies by submitting something through their websites. I believe you should spend your time on this only in the following cases:

1) Your online application is a part of an established process that culminates in the employer's coming to your campus to interview you in person.

2) You are looking for an internship, and you know for a fact that the outcome of this particular application is not dependent on the employer's visiting a pre-specified list of campuses.

3) You contacted an individual, and she suggested you go to the website to apply for a particular position. At least, in this case there's a chance that the job ad was not posted just for show. Besides, if that individual is involved in the selection process, it's a point in your favor because you made her read your resume. However, if her reply was "go to our website, some jobs must be posted there", it's worthless.

4) You believe the company hires quants, and there's no way to contact any individuals working for it via LinkedIn or other social media.

A thorough Google search will provide you with the list of target companies. A good start would be to visit the websites of some Quant Finance / Financial Engineering programs. They like to brag about where their graduates work. A few links are provided below:

1) Georgia Tech QCF program:

http://www.qcf.gatech.edu/about/industryconnections.html
Keywords: *Some Firms That Use QCF*

2) Berkeley MFE program:

http://mfe.haas.berkeley.edu/careers/placement.html
Keywords: *berkeley financial engineering placement reports*

3) Carnegie Mellon MSCF program:

http://tepper.cmu.edu/master-in-computational-finance/your-career/recruiting-partners/index.aspx
Keywords: *MSCF Employment Report*

4) "Helpful links" section of the home page of Patrick Lyons, PhD:

http://www.patlyons.com/links/Finance.htm

Keywords: *homepage of Patrick Lyons, PhD*

5) Hoovers website:

http://www.hoovers.com/

where you can search companies by keywords. I don't think it's worth paying for it, but your university library may have free access.

This will give you a fairly large list of companies, but, guess what, all of them can be contacted through the people who work there. That is, if you use appropriate search options on LinkedIn while looking for individuals (without specifying the company name), you are likely to cover those institutions anyway.

Hedge funds are different from the bigger names because they are small, secretive, and poorly represented by websites and even LinkedIn. Therefore, I would recommend purchasing hedge fund lists separately. This is different from the conventional "apply-through-the-website-and-see-what-happens" way, because hedge fund databases include contact details of individuals who work there. The two major sources are:

1) Hedgefund.Net:

www.hedgefund.net

It provides access to thousands of hedge funds located all over the world. You can obtain access to hedge fund contact information at about $200 a year. Advanced search options allow one to search by location, trading strategy, performance measures, assets under management, and many more.

2) HedgeFundJobList.com:

http://www.hedgefundjoblist.com/

The advantage of this one is that the information is organized in a convenient Excel format. Unlike hedgefund.net, it includes a special column called "Employment Inquiries Email". It is possible to purchase a list just for a particular U.S. state or region. For instance, it costs about $40 to get access to 230 funds located in Illinois. Only U.S. funds are available. If you are looking for work in the U.S., this database should be sufficient.

## 5.2 Job boards: their name is legion

Overall, job boards are not efficient, and that's exactly why I had to go through so many of them in search of value. I divide job search websites into the following three categories.

1) "Generic" websites that cater to job seekers in all industrial sectors:

CareerBuilder.com

http://www.careerbuilder.com/

Monster.com

http://www.monster.com/

Note: Monster recently acquired Yahoo Hot Jobs. Also, some sources that appear independent in reality use someone else's job search engine. To avoid duplication, pay attention to small icons saying something like "powered by Careerbuilder".

Jobcentral.com

http://www.jobcentral.com/

JobFox.com

http://www.jobfox.com

JobMagic.com

http://www.jobmagic.com/

SimpyHired.Com

http://www.simplyhired.com/

Indeed.com

http://www.indeed.com/

JobTarget.com

http://jobtargetjobfinder.com/

OdinJobs.com

http://www.odinjobs.com/

Juju search engine

http://www.job-search-engine.com/

2) Websites that cover jobs in finance and quant finance areas:

QuantSpot.com

http://quantspot.com/

Quantster.com

http://www.quantster.com/

Maths-Fi.com

http://www.maths-fi.com/

QuantFinanceJob.com

http://www.quantfinancejob.com/

QuantFinanceJobs.com (it's not the same as above)

http://quantfinancejobs.com/

QuantCode.com

http://quantcode.com/

PhDs.org

http://jobs.phds.org/

Society of Quantitative Analysts

http://sqa-us.org/

Energy Central

http://www.energycentral.com/

Global Derivatives, Job Board

http://www.global-derivatives.com/

eFinancialCareers

http://www.efinancialcareers.com/

MathFinance, Job Exchange

http://mathfinance.de/

HedgeMedia jobs

http://jobs.hedgemedia.com/

CareerBank.com

http://www.careerbank.com

The Ladders

http://www.theladders.com/

MBA-Exchange.com

http://www.mba-exchange.com/

Opalesque.com

http://www.opalesque.com/

Placing Traders

http://www.placingtraders.com/
Fins.com
http://www.fins.com/
Econ-jobs.com
http://econ-jobs.com/
RiskCareers.com
http://www.riskcareers.com/
SearchBankingJobs.com
http://searchbankingjobs.com/
Commodity Careers
http://commoditycareers.com/
Job Search Digest
http://www.jobsearchdigest.com/
Wall Street Journal – click on "Careers", "Advanced Search" and create an RSS feed:
http://online.wsj.com/home-page
Wealth Management Jobs
http://www.wealthjobs.net/

3) Websites that cater to quantitative professionals, but not necessarily within the financial sector. These, along with the "generic" sites, can be useful for implementing your "plan B" (Section 4.1).

SIAM Jobs

http://jobs.siam.org/

IcrunchData.com

http://www.icrunchdata.com/

Data Shaping

http://www.datashaping.com/

MathJob.com

http://mathjob.com/

MathJobs.org

http://www.mathjobs.org/jobs

EIMS Employment Information
http://eims.ams.org/jobs

PhysicsToday.org
http://www.physicstoday.org/jobs/

GetMathematicsJobs.com
http://www.getmathematicsjobs.com/

GetStatisticsJobs.com
http://www.getstatisticsjobs.com/

Dice.com
http://www.dice.com/

StatCareers.com
http://www.statscareers.com/

AnalyticBridge.com
http://www.analyticbridge.com/

MarketResearchCareers.com
http://www.marketresearchcareers.com/

KDNuggets Data Mining Jobs
http://www.kdnuggets.com/jobs/

SAS jobs
http://sas-jobs.com/

Not all of the websites above allow one to post a resume. To receive updates, the best option is to compose a search alert that would deliver the appropriate postings to your mailbox on a regular basis. Creating an RSS feed is another option. Some websites do not provide either, so you'll have to check for updates manually every once in a while. The ability to search by keywords and create alerts somewhat erases the boundaries between quant and non-quant websites. Monster.com, SimplyHired.com, Indeed.com and a few more "generic" ones are so huge that they include a decent number of openings that look similar to what you can get from the specialized quant boards. I will talk more about exploiting job boards in Section 7.

### 5.3 In-person networking and its ROI

The organizations that arrange networking events for quants are:
1) International Association of Financial Engineers, IAFE :
http://iafe.org/
IAFE organizes and endorses numerous networking events. They mostly take place in the US, but the host countries also include UK, Italy, France and Canada.  IAFE also holds the "National Financial Mathematics Career Fair" each fall. It is open only to full-time students who are about to graduate from a pre-specified list of universities. They submit CVs in advance and then, if the employer is interested, the students get interviewed at the fair.
2) QWAFAFEW Association:
http://qwafafew.org/
QWAFAFEW has many chapters in the U.S. and its networking events span a larger number of U.S. cities than IAFE gatherings.
3) Society for Industrial and Applied Mathematics, SIAM:
www.siam.org
which organizes "Conference on Financial Mathematics and Engineering" every other year. The next one is scheduled for summer 2012 in Minnesota, USA. Unfortunately, I find it too academic for the purposes of job search. You should always look through the list of participants of such conferences to make sure there are enough of them who actually work in the industry. It may be possible to find contact details of the participants without having to attend the conference, express interest in their research, and subsequently include them in your network.
4) Society of Quantitative Analysts:
http://sqa-us.org/
I haven't attended their events myself. As far as I could gather from the website, they are held in NYC only.

In all of the associations, membership for students is quite cheap, but the problem is that the events are held in large cities that can be far away from where you live. Apparently, it doesn't make much sense to spend about $600 to shake 10-20 hands when you can buy contact info of all hedge funds in the

US for a smaller amount. Of course, in-person networking is good for one's communication skills, but there must be a cheaper way to take care of that problem (Section 8).

One may say that in-person conversation is more efficient than the online thing, but that's far from obvious for me. On LinkedIn, the recipient of your invitation can see your full professional profile. It's hard to convey that much information during a typical in-person exchange at a live gathering. As a result, the "quality" of your "live" connections can hardly be any higher than that of your LinkedIn contacts whom you never met in person.

## 5.4 Do not be a prey: exploiting headhunters

To put it mildly, the business of quant headhunting has yet to reach its Golden Age. The unscrupulous behavior of quant headhunters is well documented on the Wilmott.com ([www.wilmott.com](www.wilmott.com)) forum. Search for topics with "headhunter" or "recruiter" in the topic title, and you'll find numerous examples of how they can screw the job seeker (here I don't mean it in the literal sense, but read on). Unfortunately, it's not the worst part of the story: the real problem is that even good headhunters (who do exist) are not helpful for a DC.

During my job search in 2008-2010, I talked to well over 100 headhunters and actually sent my CV to at least 40 who appeared the most credible. Some of these people were recommended to me, and I am sure they are good professionals… but none of them delivered. They could not even land the initial phone interviews with the employer, let alone something that would result in a job offer.

The only time I secured a phone interview through a headhunter was quite instructive. I initiate contact with headhunter A because someone recommends A as a good professional. Headhunter A says he has ties with XYZ bank, and promises to let me know as soon as XYZ has an opening. A few days later, I get a call from a previously unfamiliar headhunter B. Headhunter B introduces himself and says that there's an opening at XYZ. I don't want A and B to clash, so I call A and ask him to contact XYZ. He calls me back all excited because, indeed, XYZ has an open position now. Essentially, I did A's work for him. That anecdote only confirmed my conviction that one should be one's own headhunter. How to become one is exactly what this manual is about.

Since headhunters manage to stay in business somehow, I can speculate that they earn their living by placing "advantaged" candidates, not DCs. Why, then, do they get in touch with and accept resumes from DCs? Your guess is as good as mine. In all this time, I have met only one person who was honest enough to say: "Sorry, I can't help you. You'll be better off looking for work on your own".

That being said, it won't hurt to get acquainted with a few presumably decent headhunters and try to use them during the initial stage of your job search (Section 7). Naturally, a personal reference is the best way to do it, and, as soon as you connect with a few experienced quants, you can ask them for advice. Failing that, you can do a LinkedIn search and choose the individuals with good recommendations (one can sort the search results by the number of recommendations). Talk to them in advance and see if they satisfy some basic requirements. The headhunter must agree to keep you updated on where your resume goes, and then it's your job to make sure there are no conflicts. You should feel free to say something like "sorry, I can't allow you to submit my CV to XYZ bank because it's been already submitted by another headhunter". If a headhunter insists on exclusivity, drop him. That person simply tries to hedge his interests at your expense.

I also discovered that headhunters can add some value to a DC's existence in the following indirect ways:

1) Headhunters, no matter how bad, have very developed LinkedIn networks. Connecting with a headhunter on LinkedIn is always a good idea because of the boost it gives to the number of your $2^{nd}$ degree connections.

2) The term "headhunter jokes" traditionally refers to anecdotes about a job candidate who wears a parrot-colored tie for an interview, eats French onion soup with his bare hands, and brags about his sex life when asked "What is your greatest achievement?". In the quant space, the tables are turned, and sharing stories of headhunters' blunders can be a successful small talk topic. Quants are diverse in terms of educational and cultural backgrounds, but being subject to dumb-witted "recruiting professionals" is one thing they are likely to share.

Here's my humble contribution to the pool of headhunter jokes: I informed this "talent acquisition professional" that I would prefer a position in the Midwest (e.g., Chicago). Next thing I know, she calls me back asking if I want to move to Hong Kong. Apparently, she had a problem distinguishing between the Midwest and the Far East.

3) If you read Wilmott.com, you know that headhunters themselves call

each other "pimps". Still, I never thought they can have anything to do with the candidate's sex life. Boy, was I wrong! A real story: in the course of my last job search, I got in touch with this "recruiting professional" via email. Having checked out my photo on LinkedIn, she decided to invite me for an in-person "interview", that is, a date. I am too modest to share the details here, but I'm positive it wasn't a misunderstanding. This goes to show two things: a) I am an "advantaged" job candidate, but, sadly, in terms of looks only; b) from a DC's standpoint, an average "talent acquisition professional" is more likely to be a source of carnal favors than job offers.

## 6 Beyond LinkedIn: leveraging other social media

### 6.1 Haven't lost your job yet? Join Facebook!

The very design of a typical Facebook profile suggests that professional networking is not the main goal of this social medium. In fact, Facebook has become notorious as a major "job losing tool".  To find out more, try the following keywords:

Keywords: *bank intern busted by Facebook; employers look at Facebook too; employers snoop on facebook*

Again, keep in mind that contacting individuals is the core of your search strategy. I don't believe that there are many useful contacts that are absent on LinkedIn but present on Facebook.

Both Facebook and LinkedIn can be used to run "ads", i.e. small advertisements that work similarly to those you see on the sidebar every time you search on Google:

Keywords: *Use Facebook Ads to Make Employers Hunt You Down*
Keywords: *Use LinkedIn Ads to Make Employers Hunt You Down*

The sources above claim the superiority of Facebook, but, at any rate, this ad-based approach is too passive for a DC. Instead of running ads like "Hi, I am Melanie. I want to work for XYZ. Can you help me?" one should make direct contact with people at XYZ, ask them if there are any openings, and have them read one's resume. I myself tried this ad-based approach by subscribing for Google AdWords. The goal was to advertise my website where my resume and other professional information were posted. Having spent about $200 on it, I found it absolutely useless. Still, I am glad I tried an unorthodox strategy that might have given me an edge, and I urge you to keep an open mind as well.

### 6.2 Twitter: chirping your way into a job?

If you get the most out of your LinkedIn account and job boards, the added value of Twitter is rather limited. It's unlikely that an individual you want in your network embraces Twitter and shuns LinkedIn. The great majority of quants in my own network do not have a Twitter account. Headhunters tend to have it, but I prefer to keep in touch with them in a more explicit and personal way (Section 7). Therefore, your Twitter network is bound to be a small subset of your LinkedIn network. LinkedIn has its own version of "tweet" called "status update", so your Twitter activity is likely to be a duplication of what you have done / are doing on LinkedIn.

I see Twitter as a tool for a concise (under 140 characters) indexing of content that can be found in full elsewhere. For instance, some companies have Twitter accounts where they post new job openings. You could get the same content without Twitter, but you'll have to fill in your profile on the company's website and set up alerts, if available. The advantage of setting up alerts is that you can specify the search criteria properly. If you just follow the company on Twitter, you are to receive all of their openings indiscriminately.

Likewise, major job boards have Twitter accounts to which they forward the content. This can result in some confusion and redundancy during you search because the name of the original resource may be different from the name of its Twitter counterpart. For instance, CommodityCareers.com and JobMagic.com (Section 5.2), are linked to the Twitter accounts named TradingJobs and NumericJobs, correspondingly.

Another example: when you use the search engine TwitJobSearch.com, you will notice that many "tweeted" job postings originate from one of the boards listed in Section 5.2. However, the idea of aggregating ads from a number of job boards is implemented in Indeed.com and similar engines. I am not sure if any value is added by "twitterizing" the content that is already available in a fairly convenient form.

You may find useful the following Twitter tools:

TwitJobSearch.com

http://www.twitjobsearch.com/

TweetMyJobs.com

http://tweetmyjobs.com/

TweetByMail.com

http://www.tweetbymail.com/

TweetByMail allows one to receive tweets via regular email, with possible filtering by keywords. It is still in the beta stage, but you can find other applications that do the same thing.

Twellow.com

http://www.twellow.com/

Twitter Search

http://search.twitter.com/

Twitter Groups

http://twittgroups.com/
TweetGrid.com
http://tweetgrid.com/

Overall, I believe the lack of original content and networking opportunities does not justify a significant investment of time or money in Twitter.

## 6.3 Doostang: simple folk may apply

Doostang (www.doostang.com) is a "community of over 700,000 elite professionals with inside access to thousands of jobs from top employers" which originated as a closed website for the students of the top US colleges and MBA schools. About 50% of Doostang members work in the Finance & Investment industry. The exclusivity of this network was protected: one could join only if invited by a current member. Then, the restriction was abolished and anyone can join for free now. Upgrading to a $40-a-month Premium account is the next option.

According to my research in 11/2010, the exclusivity of Doostang is a thing of the past. I used Doostang's "People Search" to find 30 quants working in NYC, and 26 of them turned out to have LinkedIn profiles. The remaining 4 people didn't appear to be "exclusive", high-flying professionals compared to the other 26.

Incidentally, Doostang limits the number of searches per month, but it's not a problem since one can bookmark searched profiles and return to them later. The main advantage of Doostang is the possibility of sending a free message to any Doostang member, which can be used to extend one's LinkedIn network.

Doostang has its own job search engine, and, as a Premium member, you can view "premium" jobs that cannot be viewed by Basic members. It may be worth trying because:

1) The search results seem to include ads posted by employers as opposed to headhunters (see Section 7 for more).

2) If you decide to apply, Doostang provides some convenient interface for that.

3) Although the content of these ads may be found somewhere else (Indeed.com, Juju.com), it might make sense to outsource the task of searching and aggregating that information to Doostang.

There is a way to avoid paying. As of 10/2010, if you a free member subscribed to job alerts, you will get emails with the visible position title and the name of employer who posted a "premium" ad. Being a premium member allows you to read the ad itself, but it's not necessary. In many cases, Doostang will simply redirect you to the employer's website to apply. As soon as you know the hiring company and the position title, it's better to contact the company's quants or HR person directly via LinkedIn.

## 6.4 Bloomberg: a truly exclusive network

By "Bloomberg" I refer not to the website www.bloomberg.com , but to a Bloomberg terminal. It is a computer workstation that consists of a regular display and a multicolored keyboard with a number of functional keys. A number of U.S. universities (even some that are considered 2nd tier) have it in the library to supply the students and professors with financial data.

Bloomberg interface is rather convoluted, so I only give general directions here. First of all, you can access the "Jobs" section, which I don't find more helpful than the websites specified in Section 5.2. As virtually all other job boards, it is infested with headhunter ads. However, there is an opportunity to expand your network of individuals. First of all, you can search one by name, and, if one has a Bloomberg profile, you'll be able to see it, with email address and all. Since access to the terminal costs about $1000 a month, Bloomberg inadvertently created a truly exclusive social network.

Secondly, you can find lots of information about money managers who work in hedge- and mutual funds. In particular, there is this "Hedge Fund Home Page" where you can screen hedge funds by geographical location, strategy, and so on. Note that some of that information could be derived from the sources I mentioned in Section 5.1, such as Hedgefund.net.

## 6.5 FinRoad: a quiet paradise

The founders of FinRoad.com apparently wanted to create a network for financial professionals that would "remove the noise of huge business networks" like LinkedIn. At this point, there is very little noise indeed, simply because the number of members was about 20,000 as of 05/2010.

To assess FinRoad's potential, I decided to search for all members who are employed by hedge funds in NYC and London, *without* specifying the position type. As of 11/2010, the numbers of hits were about 80 and 50, correspondingly. Given the inevitable intersection of FinRoad and LinkedIn, even the time spent on filling in FinRoad profile is not going to pay off. I recommend you perform a similar "sanity check" every time you are about to invest time or money in newly established social media.

# 7 Time for battle: the active phase of your job search

## 7.1 Internships

Overall, quant internship opportunities for the people pursuing M.S. or Ph.D. are few and far between. Most of the openings target undergrads or MBAs. The few publicly available quant intern openings are associated with major banks (Section 5.1). There are three ways of searching for internships:

1) Given the list of potential employers, one can monitor their websites manually and apply as soon as there's a corresponding opening.

2) As soon as a bank posts an opening on its website, it can be extracted and brought to you by some job search engines, such as Indeed.com and Doostang.com.

3) The best way is to exploit the network of individuals that you hopefully created in advance. Headhunters have nothing to do with internships, so don't bother with them.

Although some banks can hire interns all year round, you have to be aware of the following seasonal schedule many large banks are accustomed to. Suppose you are interested in summer 2010 internship. First, a bank accepts internship applications through its website and this may start *as early as July 2009*. Next, bank representatives visit the applicant's campus sometime between September and December 2009 to interview the candidate in person. Internship offers are extended in February – March of 2010. The list of visited campuses is known in advance. If your university does not belong to it, don't waste your time applying. Fortunately, not all banks (even major ones) are thus restricted. Also, keep in mind your own time limitations: e.g. graduate teaching assistants may have to inform the university in advance about their summer plans, and non-residents of the US may need extra time for the intern application to be processed.

I myself had no luck applying to major banks (although I know some DCs who did), and both of my internships have been with relatively small hedge funds. Needless to say, I relied on my network of individuals to spread the word by sending "regular" emails. I had no LinkedIn account back then, so I only managed to pull it off because of relatively low unemployment rate at the time. Therefore, it's imperative that you create and exploit a LinkedIn network as early as possible. Here's an example of Linked Inmail that may be helpful:

Dear Martin:

Forgive me for not using your full name – you are my $3^{rd}$ degree connection and I can't see it.

I came across your LinkedIn profile and I was wondering if you could help me. I am a graduate student at XXX University where I study Quantitative Finance. At this point, I have already taken a number of relevant courses. I also possess certain software skills. If you or someone you know may be interested in a summer intern, please forward this message accordingly.

I would also be happy to see you in my network. Please send me an invitation on abc@gmail.com or let me know your email, and I will invite you myself. If you are not interested, please do NOT reply to this Inmail.

Regards,

name

    Note that my purpose here is twofold: a) find an internship; b) expand my network, which is probably even more important than a). This is a rule you should follow whenever you communicate with people in the course of your search: use every opportunity to obtain more connections. Every time I get an email from a professional who is not yet in my network, I use my knowledge of his email address to send him an invitation. In that sense, there's no such thing as a failed job search, because, if your network grows, you are bound to have better chances next time.

    As a DC, I'd rather bet on the "hidden" internship market as opposed to crowded application portals of bigger name banks. The two internships I got were NEVER advertised anywhere. The second one was with a hedge fund whose publicly available website consisted of a single page saying that only its investors could login and see the rest. To tell you more, I didn't know about the existence of those two funds until I got a reply from them: in each case, my email was forwarded to them by someone, and, to this day, I have no idea who that someone was (please accept my belated thanks, comrades!). This goes to show the importance of having a large network of contacts who may not know you in person and yet turn out to be helpful.

    In my search, I measure a rough "response rate" as follows. Each sent email, LinkedIn message, online application, etc, counts as one "action". Queries sent to individuals working for the same company are considered distinct "actions". The response rate is the average number of actions one has to take to obtain one initial phone interview. During my internship search periods, the unemployment rate in the US fluctuated around 4-5%, and, on average, I would get one phone interview per 80 actions. In 2009-2010, the unemployment being 8-10%, it required about 120 "actions" to get one response. In the most favorable scenario, one out of three initial phone interviews leads to a job offer. You can play with this rough Binomial model yourself. It's obvious that, even in the very best case, you have to take a minimum of 250 actions to have a decent chance. This applies to both internships and long-term positions.

## 7.2 Permanent positions

An important question is when one should start looking. There are some commonly known seasonal patterns. For instance, hiring is high in April-May when freshly minted university graduates get jobs (for long-term positions, the hiring schedule is similar to that for internships). Little goes on in December, and January is known as the "musical chairs" season: bank employees collect bonuses for the year and it's the best time for them to switch jobs.

The timing depends on what job search tools you are using. Contacting individuals in your network can be done within a short time frame. If there are any job offers, you are more likely to receive them simultaneously, which is a good thing. With more conventional job search tools, it takes much longer. To find my first permanent position, I started my search about 7 months prior to graduation. Now that my network is much larger, I can finish the search of comparable quality within 2 ½ months.

I am going to recommend a certain chronological order of steps, but you have to decide for yourself how much time to spend on each.

1) By the time you start, you should already have a list of quant headhunters with whom you are going to work (Section 5.4), and now it's time to send your resume to them. I would say it's ok to work with 2-5 headhunters simultaneously.

Occasionally (once in a fortnight is ok) you should remind the headhunter(s) about your existence and /or supply them with an updated copy of your resume. Do put very little faith in headhunters. I wouldn't give them more than a month before proceeding to the next step.

At the same time, start subscribing to job boards, search engines and other resources that will supply you with job postings via email or RSS (Section 5.2). Post your resume online so that it is represented on all three kinds of websites, "generic", "quant finance" and "quantitative". Try to prevent your resume from being harvested by "recruiting professionals" and sent somewhere without your knowledge. It is preferable to post it in PDF as opposed to Word, because headhunters need to delete one's contact information.

The most noticeable effect of posting your resume online will be a number of phone calls from "stray" headhunters. You have to realize that a headhunter who initiates contact with you cannot be a coveted professional. Her "ties" with the quant industry are probably not stronger than yours, and the way she works is similar to what you are already doing. The difference is that when she contacts an employer, the latter knows he will have to pay her to hire you. Hence, if you cut her out of the chain, you have a better chance because the employer will be more willing to hire you "for free". Therefore, the best course of action is to inform the headhunter that you already have one, and politely invite her into your LinkedIn network to "keep in touch in the future".

I have to admit – that's not what I did in the past. I would start working with 3-5 headhunters and end up with 20. It was very comforting to hope I could outsource my headache to these nice, well-spoken, encouraging individuals. It gave me a false sense of security: if so many people are busy looking for work on my behalf, how could it fail? And even if it did fail, I had plenty of scapegoats to blame. Do not repeat my mistakes: the sooner you recognize that you are on your own, the better.

2) Start contacting individuals you can reach directly via email, free LinkedIn messages, Inmail, and other means. If you are contacting someone you don't know well in person, the content of your message should be similar to a cover letter, only shorter. The difference is that a cover letter should be tied to a particular job description to highlight how good of a fit you are. Here, however, you don't know if there's an opening at all, so your self-introduction should be shorter and vaguer. An example is shown below.

Dear Mr. Davis:

I obtained your email address from Hedgefund.net and I was wondering if you could help me. I am about to graduate with a PhD in Quantitative Finance from XXX University and I am looking for a position of quantitative developer / researcher.

Apart from my excellent quantitative background and good software skills, I have had industry exposure working as an intern for VVV Capital Management, an hedge fund located in CT.

If you know of a good opening, please forward this message to an interested party.

Thank you for your time and consideration.

Yours sincerely,

name

,

If you have a deadline for obtaining a job offer, it's natural to pace yourself in a way that allows you to get in touch with all of your connections a few weeks before the deadline. LinkedIn Inmails are going to be a large part of the process, and it's a good idea to subscribe to a plan and accumulate some Inmails in advance (Inmails expire after 90 days). As always, remember to use your job search as a tool to expand your network.

Keep an accurate record of all people and companies you interact with. If you are a paid LinkedIn member, you can place other people's profiles in different folders you create by using "Profile Organizer". It helps sort the profiles by geographical location, whether the person has already been contacted, and so on. The system always shows you whether a given profile belongs to one of your folders. Likewise, it shows whether an Inmail has been sent to that person from you, which is good for avoiding duplication.

While contacting individuals is the major instrument in your toolkit, do not forget about other avenues. At this point, you must be receiving a constant stream of job-related content thanks to subscriptions you made in Step 1). Some websites have no alerts / RSS, or RSS may be malfunctioning, so you'll have to check the content manually.

When you look at a job description, the first thing is to determine whether it's been posted by an employer or by a headhunter. Usually, a headhunter's ad omits the employer's name and sounds like "A major investment bank is looking for a quantitative researcher…" and it is posted under the name of the headhunting firm, e.g. "XXX Associates". I also noticed a couple of savvy headhunting firms that picked their names in such a way as to pass themselves for actual financial institutions. Headhunter-generated "job openings" must be ignored. If you are tempted to yield to them, I direct you back to Step 1). Unfortunately, most of what you are going to see will consist of that kind of garbage.

If you come across a decent job ad, it should be interpreted as a sign that the company may be hiring. Your first step should be to check if you have already contacted someone from that company, and, if not, do it now. As I said in Section 5.1, I don't see much sense in applying through the website unless it's the only way to reach the employer.

# 8 What is your main weakness? Interviewing

## 8.1 A beast of six heads: types of interview questions

There are six major types of interview questions:

1) "Quantitative" questions that require some specific knowledge of Calculus, Probability, Linear Algebra, Financial Math, etc. Examples: taking indefinite integrals, solving PDEs, pricing a European call option via binomial method.

Most of the items in References are devoted to such questions, the recent being Zhou (2008) and Joshi (2008A). Lots of quantitative questions are available in the "Brainteaser" forum of Wilmott.com. However, the problem is that the number of covered topics is so large that it is impossible to stay sharp on all of them at once. That means you have to be able to predict, roughly, what areas are going to be relevant during a given job interview. First of all, you have to inquire whether the interview is behavioral or quantitative. For a quantitative one, you can narrow down the list of possible topics by using the information from:

a) Job description

b) Company profile, especially if it is a small one

c) Profiles of people who are going to interview you. Ask the names of these people in advance, look them up on LinkedIn or Google, and use some common sense. For instance, if your interviewer has a PhD in Statistics, PDE questions are not likely, as opposed to Time Series or, say, multiple linear regression stuff. If he is a Finance PhD, then forget about Measure Theory and Stochastic Calculus and focus on more down-to-earth questions about equity options, IR products, etc.

d) If you use the company name as a keyword, concrete interview questions can sometimes be found on Wilmott.com forum.

2) Software questions (Section 9).

3) "Behavioral" questions, a.k.a. "soft" questions or "competency questions" (the latter term used by Morgan Stanley). Examples: "Why should we hire you?", "What is your main weakness?"

4) Abstract brain-teasers. These questions do not require any specific knowledge like in 1) and yet they try to test one's intelligence. Example: "You are given two fuses. It is known that each of them burns for one hour, but their rate of burning is not constant. For instance, if you split such fuse into two parts of identical length, you can't be sure that each part will burn

for exactly 30 minutes. How do you measure 45 minutes?". Counting questions, e.g. "What is 17 cubed?" also fall into this category.

5) "Case questions" where you are required to solve a particular business problem. The claimed purpose is to "get you talking" and assess the quality of your thinking process. These questions are described well in Jiu (2010).

6) Questions about the current state of financial market, e.g.: "What is the oil price today (1 month ago, 1 year ago)?", "Who is the current Fed chairman?". More examples can be found in Crack (2009) and Joshi (2008A).

Type 3) and 4) questions are more dangerous for a quant because they are often not what they seem. It may appear odd that I consider them together, but that will be clarified in Section 8.4. The current quant job search literature glosses over them because it is assumed that communication skills are not that important for a quant. While this approach may work for "advantaged" job seekers, a DC cannot afford it. Think about it: if you are a DC competing against someone from a more famous school, what factors can tip the scales in your favor? You have lower salary expectations, that's a good one. What else? The only other thing I can think of is your being less nerdy than your MIT–bred competition.

To develop your communication skills, I suggest you find some (on-campus) activity where you get to talk to people a lot. For instance, joining the local branch of Toastmasters International (www.toastmasters.org) was what I did. Attending quant networking events is also good unless it costs you much money.

Interviewing over the phone is a lot more difficult, and, if English is your second language, it may seem an absolutely impossible endeavor. I still don't get the intonation well, which causes problems with taking turns while talking: someone asks me a question, I answer it, and then follows a 20-second silence because, for some reason, the opponent thinks I'm not finished answering. What I learned to do is to finish my thoughts with small *verbal* clues so that the opponent knows that it's now his turn. I'm not going to share those here, but I suggest you explain the problem to a native English speaker and ask him what he would use in that situation. I got lots of phone practice from talking to headhunters, but, since such talks are pretty short, you have to go through over 100 of them (as I did). The only cheap solution I can think of is to purchase an accent reduction tool. For instance, on Amazon.com go to "Books" and use "American accent" keywords to search by the title.

Answering Type 3) and 4) questions is impossible without your understanding of what is really going on in your opponent's head. If you take the question literally, as if it were Type 1) question, you are more likely to fail. Sections 8.2-8.4 below are dedicated to "deciphering" and answering such questions.

## 8.2 Behavioral interviewing: a happy marriage

John and Susan Rogers have been married for 15 years. Some of their friends think they are a great couple; others say they don't care for each other all that much. Oddly enough, John and Susan agree that both of these things are true: from their perspective, a certain degree of mutual indifference is what makes a relationship stable. Each of them is almost certain that the other one has had affairs on the side, but neither of them lost any sleep over that. What they do care for is being civil and tactful to each other. Inconvenient questions are carefully avoided, and, even when such a question slips out, both John and Susan know what a true gentleman or lady is supposed to answer.

For instance, Susan comes home from work more shiny-eyed and excited than usual (in fact, usually she's not excited at all). John suspects that the reason for that is something that Susan did with her hot young assistant behind the closed doors of her office. However, when John asks Susan how her day was, he certainly doesn't expect to hear any of that. Susan understands the rules, too, being considerate of her husband. There is a lot of mutual consideration going on.

If this good couple sounds familiar to you, then you'll easily understand what behavioral interviewing is about. The difference is that your opponent is now entitled to asking provocative, edgy questions, but your part remains the same: a considerate spouse. I suggest you avoid sounding even slightly negative or critical of anything, especially your former job experience. For instance, consider the following exchange that took place between myself and a headhunter:

*I:* My last job was about … (here I describe my job duties).

*Headhunter:* This kind of work doesn't sound interesting for a PhD like yourself.

*I:* That's true, but I tried to make it more interesting by using the company's data to perform some research in order to publish a paper in the end. *(I am being proud of myself here. I tried to "be proactive and creative",*

*Headhunter:* How did it go?

*I:* Not too well. My former boss was not very supportive of it.

*Headhunter:* Why, because you didn't finish projects on time?

Wait a second. Did I ever mention any projects that were not finished on time? No, I didn't. Secondly, even if there were such projects, why does the headhunter assume that it had something to do with my research work? I did it on my own time.

That's the attitude that you should expect when you say something negative: you words can very well be twisted and make you look like a jerk. Let's erase and rewind. This time, I am going to be an upbeat, supportive, and considerate spouse:

*I:* My last job was about … (here I describe my job duties).

*Headhunter:* This kind of work doesn't sound interesting for a PhD like yourself.

*I:* Actually, I think it was very useful for me. I managed to learn a lot of practical things pertaining to XYZ modeling. You see, there are many aspects of XYZ which cannot be learned at school, but such details are crucial when you do XYZ modeling in an industrial setting. I am lucky that I managed to get that experience.

*Headhunter:* Great! Now that you are open to explore new opportunities, let me see what I can do for you…

I tried the considerate spouse version and, guess what, it works much better. When I switch on the "considerate" mode, I can almost hear the opponent sigh with relief about my being so positive. Sometimes you may feel that your opponent is fine with you saying something negative, but be careful: it is likely to be a trap. In the example above, the headhunter suggested that maybe my last job was not so interesting, and I fell for it. Again, try to think of it in terms of John and Susan Rogers: when Susan says something like "Maybe I didn't look my best last night at the party..." or even "I think you are cheating on me...", what does she expect to hear from John?

Therefore, I came to deconstructing each behavioral question as follows:

a) Determine the *nominal*, "formal" meaning of the question. This is what your opponent *claims* he wants (or doesn't want) to know.

b) Determine the *real* purpose of the question. This is what your opponent *really* wants (or doesn't want) to know.

c) Determine the things that you are (not) supposed to say to keep the opponent happy.

Below I break apart some behavioral questions whose nominal meaning is most likely different from the real one.

1) Why shouldn't we hire you?

a) Nominal meaning: they want to know if there are any deficiencies in your professional background that can make you a bad fit for this position.

b) Real meaning: they have already seen your CV and talked to you for a while. At this point, they are fairly aware of possible misfits. If you think they are asking you to open their eyes to something they might have missed, think again. The real reason for asking this question is to assess how badly you want the job.

c) What not to say: do not try to compose the list of your deficiencies. On the other hand, the job description may contain a requirement that you don't satisfy now and will never care to learn, e.g., the ability to manage people. You should assess whether that item can get you fired shortly after you are hired, and, if yes, it makes sense to bring it up.

What to say: if the job description has none of the deal-breakers mentioned above, your answer should be: "I can't think of a reason why you shouldn't hire me. I believe I'm a great fit for this position".

2) Why did you leave your last position?

This question may seem irrelevant for an entry-level DC, but remember that "entry-level" means less than 2 years of experience after graduation, and lots of things may happen within those 2 years. Most importantly, this question is probably the most devious of all, and looking into it will give you insight into other questions as well.

I believe that here one should be aware and beware of the following terminology:

"fired" – means your performance was unsatisfactory, the company got rid of you and hired someone else instead.

"laid off" – regardless of your performance, the company decided to liquidate your position altogether, e.g., because of recession.

"let go" – this term has a neutral meaning and can refer to either of the above.

Let's consider two scenarios. Scenario 1 : you were fired or laid off, a.k.a. let go.

a) Nominal meaning: they want to know if you did something bad at your last job and they expect you to be honest about it. If you recognize your mistakes, you may deserve a second chance.

b) Real meaning: they want to know how tactful and considerate you are. Believe it or not, they don't care to hear what really happened between you and your last employer. If you find this odd, I again refer you to John and Susan Rogers and their stable, fulfilling, committed relationship.

c) What to say: first, if you were fired and there's an opportunity to present this as a lay-off, by all means do it. In the US, your past employer is forbidden to disclose whether you were fired, laid off, or left voluntarily. All she can share is your past job title and the dates of employment.

A short "I was laid off because of recession" is a perfectly acceptable answer which sounds plausible if there's a real recession. Also, you probably have been the "youngest" employee and the rule "last hired, first fired" makes your story even more believable. The company might have decided to downsize for a number of reasons, and, understandably, you must have been very vulnerable in that respect.

If you were fired and there's no way to get around that it was about your performance, highlight the differences between your previous role and the position you are now pursuing. Say that the job description you were originally presented with and the actual role had many discrepancies and that both your employer and you soon realized that you were not the ideal fit for the position. You can always say that the decision was mutual and that you came to an understanding that it was better that they find someone else for the position.

What not to say: do not try to defend yourself. If you believe that you were fired unfairly, saying so is the worst thing you can do. You are considered married to your last employer until you find a new one, and being a considerate spouse is still your sacred duty.

Scenario 2 : you left voluntarily.

a) Nominal meaning: They want to know what was it you didn't like about your last position, because the same circumstances may recur at their firm and, in that case, you are not a good fit for them.

b) Same as for Scenario 1.

c) What to say: if you didn't like something about your last firm, it's your job to make sure you won't get into that again. However, expressing that in terms "I really hated doing X and I won't do it again" during a job interview is inconsiderate of your last employer. Instead, your answer should be more like: "My experience with X was a useful one, and I enjoyed working with all those nice people, but now I would like to find work that is more to do with Y, because I want to grow as a professional".

Keep in mind that the hiring manager will always view it as a red flag that you left without having secured another position. You can always say that you felt it was dishonest continuing in the position when you were looking elsewhere. You can also say that looking for a new job is a full-time job in itself and you felt it was unfair to your employer that you constantly come up with fake excuses when you need to go on an interview.

What not to say: again, be considerate. Even if your ex-spouse (former co-workers) deserved to get shot on sight, saying that aloud is not a good way to start a relationship with your new significant other.

3) How would your former boss describe you?

a) Nominal meaning: they want to know if your former boss was happy with your performance and what he thought your deficiencies were.

b) Real meaning: again, this is a test for how well you are adjusted for working in the corporate environment, which boils down to being a considerate spouse.

c) What to say: "My former boss would say that I have an excellent potential and it was too bad they couldn't keep me". Alternatively, even if you were fired because of performance, there must have been some redeeming qualities that your boss could bring up. You can say that although you were not a fit with the role as it was defined after you were hired, your boss appreciated your professionalism and understanding. Additionally, if you had at least one performance evaluation you can mention what was discussed as your strong points.

What not to say: If your boss would indeed say something negative about you, you may think that being honest about that can earn you some points with your prospective employer. However, that's not true at all: remember that, in this context, "honesty" and "inconsideration" are synonyms. If you are that straightforward, you are not likely to keep your mouth shut when your new boss does something dumb, and nobody wants that kind of employee.

4) What do your friends think of you?

a) Nominal meaning: they want a side opinion on you to find out more what kind of person you are.

b) Real meaning: this is another test for being socially smart /

considerate.

c) What to say: recall and embroider a few positive remarks that your friends made about you, but not to the point when they sound unrealistic.

What not to say: just like in Question 3), it doesn't pay to "be honest" about anything negative your friends have to say about you. Secondly, don't say something like: "My friends think I am hard-working, have a great attention to detail, and possess outstanding communication skills". Even if it's all true, your friends do not express themselves in such terms. Avoid these clichés and test all your answers with a following rule of thumb: if it sounds bombastic, it probably is. Numerous examples of such mumbo-jumbo can be found on the "Who we are" webpage of virtually all US corporations. Borrow that style and you will reap not job offers but only long, resonant, jaw-dislocating yawns.

5) How would you describe yourself?

a) Nominal meaning: they want to hear the list of your strengths from you. If you are an honest person, you may even mention a few weaknesses.

b) Real meaning: same as for questions 3) and 4).

c) What to say: this question is about you as a person. Think of a few positive features that you possess, with real examples of what you did to show them. You can borrow some from Question 4). Example: "I am intellectually curious: despite my strong quantitative background, I am also interested in the areas that are not amenable to quantitative analysis. For instance, I recently read this book on...."

What not to say: similar to Question 4). Avoid disclosing negative information and/or turning yourself into a ludicrous cliché-spitting parrot: "I am a very kind, likeable, hard-working individual with great communication skills. But, of course, humility is my major feature!"

6) What are your strengths?

This question is similar to Question 5). You can also throw in some technical skills if you can relate them to the job description and the buzzwords it contains.

An example on "non-technical" strength: "I am very good at explaining quantitative stuff to the people with no quantitative background. In particular, during my internship with XYZ bank I had to do that a lot with MBA people and even one person who had a B.A. in English Literature."

7) What are your weaknesses?

Question 1) is about your weaknesses in the context of a particular job description and part or all of it can be used for answering Question 7) also. The difference is that while "I am sure I am a great fit" works for Question 1), answering "I have no weaknesses" for Question 7) doesn't sound good at all.

For a DC, a good answer could be a lack of industrial experience, e.g.: "My internship at QQQ bank was a great experience and all, but I wish I had more industrial exposure. I am determined to eliminate that flaw as soon as possible". Since they are perfectly aware of your lack of experience, you can answer the question and do no harm to yourself.

What not to say: a popular suggestion is to turn this question into describing your strengths instead. However, "My main weakness is that I am way too hard-working" or something along those lines has become so overused that you should just forget about it. Also, answers like "Chocolate is the major love and weakness of my life!" means that you are either trying to be funny (and failing) or don't understand what the question is about.

8) Why do you want to work for our company, XYZ?

a) Nominal meaning: they want to know why you are interested in XYZ in particular, because, if you have some specific reasons, you are likely to be a good fit.

b) Real meaning: How badly do you want to get this position?

As an entry-level candidate, you are very unlikely to have special information to justify your choice of XYZ over another similar company, XYS. Of course, the interviewer is aware of that, so why ask the question in the first place?

What I think is going on: if you are a "serious" candidate, you are expected to have done some research on XYZ. Most likely, any publicly available information will probably be useless for choosing XYZ over XYS, but that's beside the point: if you haven't spent/wasted a chunk of your time on research, you failed to show strong interest in the position. This may seem odd to you, but, once hired, you'll have to do your share of meaningless things, so you might as well get used to it in advance.

c) What to say: Most likely, the information on the corporate websites of XYZ, XYS and similar firms will boil down (pun intended) to the same cliché soup: "Our most valuable asset is our people", "we provide outstanding returns to our investors", "teamwork-oriented environment", "integrity and creativity", etc. Is it me or all US companies hire the very same PR person to come up with this concoction? You have to try to find something that doesn't put your opponent to sleep as fast as that bland potion.

Example: "… I am also interested in XYZ because of its leading position in the QuantFinance industry. In particular, I came across this article online, and, as it turns out, XYZ was the very firm that pioneered the RRR quantitative trading strategy, which is now used by many hedge funds and investment banks."

What not to say: avoid saying / implying that you don't see much difference between XYZ and similar firms. For instance, saying that you are interested because of this particular job description sounds ok, but it also implies that, if XYS posted a similar position, you would be just as excited. You don't want to create that impression.

9) Where do you see yourself five years from now?

a) Nominal meaning: they want to know if your long-term professional goals are in line with what you can achieve inside the company.

b) Real meaning: If you take this question literally, it's meaningless. Presumably, the company expects you to stay with them for the next five years. During my job searches, I went through over a thousand LinkedIn profiles, and very few people in the (quant) finance sector had a job they kept that long. The financial meltdown of 2008-? made this question especially laughable, and yet it is asked anyway – to see how badly you want the job. Just like with marriage, you are supposed to show commitment, to prove that you are into this deal for the long haul, despite the 50% divorce rate (in the US).

c) What to say: transform this question into how you can grow in and with this particular company, XYZ, in the next five years. Example: "Within next five years, I hope to gain lots of field knowledge about XYZ's business and become a recognized quantitative expert at XYZ".

What not to say: "Are you kidding? I'm sure that, in five years, both you and me will have changed jobs, possibly more than once!". This is equivalent to saying "The overall divorce rate is 50%, so let's get married, give it a year or two, and see what happens". Unless you think (or, at least, claim) that you are going to be with your spouse forever, you future spouse (employer) will be right in not marrying (hiring) you.

10) What distinguishes you from other people we might hire for this position?

a) Nominal meaning: they want you to perform comparative analysis and emphasize your advantages over the rest of candidates, if any.

b) Real meaning: How badly do you want to get this position?

Apparently, the opponent is not providing you with a stack of other candidates' resumes, so it's impossible to answer this question literally when you have no information about other candidates. You can flatter them by saying that you have no doubt they have received numerous applications from top people since it's such an interesting opportunity. That being said, you are 100% confident that *you* are a perfect fit for the position – and then talk about that at length.

c) What to say: compile your answer based on the answers you prepared for Questions 5) and 6). If you feel like there is a strong point in your resume, emphasize it, because there's a good chance that your opponent hasn't read your CV at all. If you have to say something that is not in your CV, it's even better. In my case, I could say: "Being from a different culture, I have a knack of adapting easily to new social and professional environments". In reality, such knack is unlikely to be unique, because many of US quants are foreigners, but it still sounds good. If the opponent responds with something like "no, we have lots of candidates like you" (a real story), it simply means he's trying to haze you (see Section 8.4).

What not to say: do not take this question literally. Answers like "I think I'm an average candidate with average skills" or "You have to describe other candidates first" are not going to work.

11) Don't you think you are overqualified for this position?

This question is very similar to Question 1). If they were sure you are overqualified, they wouldn't be talking to you in the first place.

What to say: if you really want the job, show how enthusiastic and modest you are, e.g. "Well, my PhD may be a bit of an overkill, but I am sure that, if hired, I can still learn a lot of things I had no chance of learning at school. I am convinced that education without practical experience doesn't mean much anyway, so feeling overqualified won't be an issue for me."

What not to say: "You are right, this position is well below my level, but you may as well hire me and capitalize on my stellar quantitative skills. Until I find a more fitting job, that is." Again, back to John and Susan Rogers: imagine that John says: "I don't think I deserve you, Susan. You are so pretty and intelligent, and I (sigh) – I am just a plain country boy." What kind of reply does he expect from Susan?

12) Describe a situation in which you had to be honest.

a) Nominal meaning: they want to make sure of your integrity.

b) Real meaning: they want to see if you are socially smart and your level of nerdiness is below a certain acceptable threshold. Also, it's hard to answer this question unless you are a good liar – the skill highly prized by some financial institutions.

c) Example of what to say: "While looking for a job, I believe the best strategy is to be honest about the skill set I have to offer. I believe I am not doing myself or others any favors by misrepresenting my professional profile."

What not to say: avoid mentioning any past misconduct that is likely to terminate your interview process. That's exactly what the opponent is fishing for. Apparently, an invitation to "be honest" is almost always a bait.

13) Describe a situation in which you had to lie.

a) Same as for question 12).

b) Same as for question 12)

c) What to say: I don't think that describing some professional situation is safe enough. If the opponent knows you could lie then, how can she be sure you haven't told a bunch of lies during this interview? Therefore I would make the answer personal: e.g., you probably have happened to be dishonest in the past to protect the feelings of your friends or relatives.

What not to say: same as for question 12). Do realize that the opponent is fishing for something to remove your name from the list of candidates.

14) Walk me through your CV.

I don't believe this question has a dual meaning, except you have to realize that the interviewer may not have read your resume at all. If you have a phone interview with two or more people, at least one of them haven't read it and/or got a copy of it about 5 seconds before the interview started. For this question, as well as for other questions where you describe your achievements and professional experiences, you have to add a "humanizing" feature every now and then.

What not to say: "In 2005, I worked for XYZ Capital Management, a long-short equity fund, as an intern. My work consisted of using GHG type models in order to hedge the firm's exposure. The model was implemented using Matlab, and I got quite proficient at it. Then, in 2006, I got another internship with TTY Capital Management. Since they are a fixed income hedge fund, the modeling I did was quite different from that at XYZ. This time, I used ACA interest rate model and did lots of Excel VBA and C++ programming."

While such answer is factually perfect, it sounds very boring. Below is a better version with "humanizing" stuff in italics.

What to say: "In 2005, I worked for XYZ Capital Management, a long-short equity fund, as an intern. *XYZ is located in Connecticut, and it was very refreshing to leave my Oregon campus for a while and explore a different part of the US.* My work consisted of using GHG type models in order to hedge the firm's exposure. The model was implemented using Matlab, and I got quite proficient at it. *At the same time, I managed to have some, fun, too, because of proximity to NYC where I visited Metropolitan Opera and a number of other famous places.*

Now, let me assign you some homework. Deconstruct the following question:

15) Describe the worst boss you ever had.

a) Nominal meaning:

b) Real meaning:

c) What to say:

What not to say:

In my estimate, there are about 40 "core" questions for which you must prepare answers in advance. An answer to any other question can be compiled from those 40. To learn more questions, I refer you to Crack (2009), Jiu (2010), and Joshi (2008A). The book of Leanne (2003) contains lots of behavioral questions, but the sample answers are often stuffed with clichés. They should be considered as counterexamples only.

For a quant, behavioral questions appear intimidating at first, but, as soon as you master the a,b,c) deconstruction above, it should be much easier. In the end, the HR person who interviewed you must be able to say: "I spoke with a really nice candidate today. He (she) sounds just like my husband (wife) of 15 years!"

## 8.3 The true face of your future spouse

If you are a DC looking for a job in a market as bad as that of 2009-2010, the advice on how to "choose among multiple job offers" may sound like a bad joke. Therefore, the main goal of researching your potential employer is to increase your chances of being hired and keeping the job afterwards.

As we saw in the previous section, a more or less experienced applicant can easily game his way through a behavioral interview. Likewise, the interviewer is always in the "considerate spouse" mode, unwilling to disclose anything bad about his current employer. You don't have many dates (interviews) with you future spouse (employer). During the short courtship period, it is not advisable to ask your date to give you a list of all his/her personal deficiencies and past sexual encounters. Consider the following phone conversation between myself and a member of HR department of my prospective employer (Mr. Z is the name of my potential boss):

*I:* What does it take to be a good fit for this position?

*HR person (chirping):* Well, we are looking for people who have good communication skills, and who are also hard-working and innovative!

*I:* Great... But you do realize that there is not a single firm that claims to be looking for rude, lazy, and unimaginative people? Could you tell me what's really going on in your company?

*HR person (in her normal voice, slightly hoarse):* Eh....You know what ... Ok, but let me get out of office to have a cigarette first. I'll call you back from my cell phone. (*after a couple of minutes*) Hi again. The truth is that Z is a total jerk, and it takes a special talent not to piss him off. That's what "good communication skills" are for.

*I:* Now we are talking! And what about the next quality on the list, being a hard worker?

*HR person (inhales deeply):* It's not exactly what you think. After Z's wife divorced him, he took to sitting in the office thirteen hours a day, making everyone do the same. So, even if you can finish all your work within eight hours, you'd better pretend to be busy for another four.

*I:* I see. But you do need innovative, creative people, right?

*HR person (inhales so loud I could hear it without a phone):* We say we do, but the real thing is different. In fact, the last guy who worked in this position was fired because he was too innovative for Z's taste.

*I:* It doesn't look like you are happy there. Thanks for your help and good luck in your future job search.

*HR person (lights up another one):* You are welcome. Good luck with your search, too.

Unfortunately, a conversation like that could never have happened in the real world, and it never will. The very attempt to ask something of the sort would portray you as inconsiderate. Therefore, past employees are about the only source of information about your future work environment. They can be easily found on LinkedIn, where the search options allow you to look specifically for the past employees of a given company. Once found, they can be contacted via Inmail or Jigsaw.com. Looking up the company on Wilmott.com may also help.

Needless to say, a past employee is often a disgruntled one, and, as a quant, you should adjust for that bias. However, sometimes what you learn is too weird to be a fruit of someone's fantasy. For instance, I once contacted this quant who had been employed by a prosperous hedge fund. First, he told me how much I should expect to earn if hired, which turned out to be surprisingly little considering the fund's stellar performance and its expensive geographical location. Secondly, he shared the office nickname of my potential boss: Ted Bundy, a notorious American serial killer.

## 8.4 Brain-teasers: keeping the universe in balance

It was the obvious inefficiency of "behavioral" interviewing that resulted in the rise of abstract brain-teasers. If you want the full story, I strongly recommend Poundstone (2003). In this section, I mention the most important parts of his research and amplify them with my own ideas.

Microsoft was a major proponent of brain-teasers, and Wall Street companies, in quest for the Holy Grail Of Successful Hiring, eventually adopted them as well. The claimed advantages of brain-teasers are as follows:

1) Brain-teasers often have concrete answers. It is possible to quantify the candidate by recoding the proportion of correctly solved brain-teasers. On the other hand, the "correctness" of answering behavioral questions is strongly dependent on the personal perception of the interviewer. Studies show that such perception forms within 30 seconds of talking to a candidate, and the subsequent behavioral questions and answers do not change it much.

2) In a fast-changing technological environment, it makes little sense to test for particular skills, because they turn obsolete quickly. What is more important is the ability to adapt, to "think independently" and "outside the box". Brain-teasers measure that sort of ability.

3) Along with behavioral questions, brain-teasers are well suited for young candidates with no work experience.

From my perspective, being good at brainteasers is indicative of only one thing: one's ability to solve brain-teasers. It is a knack that can be learned within 3-6 months of studying and flashed during an interview. It dissipates quickly after one is hired, since it has nothing to do with the real quant work. To acquire the knack, I refer you to Crack (2009), Joshi (2008A), Poundstone (2003), Srinivas (2010), Zhou (2008), and the "Brainteaser" forum of Wilmott.com.

Brain-teasers were never fun for me. I find counting questions especially annoying, but, at the end of the day, I don't think they are that much different from other brain-teasers. The only time I had to apply "outside-the-box" thinking was to solve the following dilemma: suppose you are asked a hard brain-teaser that you've seen before. Is it better to confess or not? Be careful: some problems are solved by very peculiar tricks. In that case, your "solution" will be very transparent to an experienced interviewer. It's not that easy to simulate the initial ignorance and the subsequent solution search process.

When you are eventually hired as a quant, you are likely to come across the following situation: your firm uses a certain quant model. Everybody knows that the model is faulty and unrealistic, but it is used anyway because: a) it does provide some needed answers, albeit incorrect; b) it is an accepted industry standard, a.k.a. "everyone else is doing it"; c) there's just no better alternative to it. I see both behavioral and brain-teaser questions as a "hiring model" of that kind. Alternatives to this crapshoot model do exist, but they are inevitably more time- and money-consuming. To find out more, check out:

Keywords: *New-Boy Network job interviews Myers*

In a certain way, however, brain-teasers do manage to improve on the low quality of the behavioral questions. Consider the following questions:

1) Do you really want to get this position? We saw that many behavioral questions boil down to this one.

2) Are you able to follow orders? That is, if your boss tells you to do something you disagree with, will you do it anyway?

3) Are you able to work under stress? Simply speaking, is it hard to piss you off?

4) Are you able to work with a "difficult" person?

As we saw in Section 8.2, it is virtually useless to ask these and similar questions directly: a reasonably smart candidate will instantly see that the expected answer is "yes" and respond with a more or less persuasive version of "yes". Instead, the interviewer can do something like this:

*Interviewer:* Your resume says you have good quantitative skills, right?

*Candidate (confidently):* Yes, I have a PhD-level background in a number of quantitative methods.

*Interviewer:* Great! Now, how much is 17 cubed?

*Candidate:* What the hell!? Are you serious?

*Interviewer (thinking):* This guy may know a thing or two about quantitative models, but he's absolutely unable to follow orders. I asked him to do one small thing I knew he wouldn't like, and he snapped. Does he really want this job? I'm being like 10% as "difficult" as many people in our firm, and he already can't stand it. There's no way he will fit into our stressful environment.

Thus, brain-teasers can serve as a "wrapper" for the behavioral questions above. In addition, some interviewers will try to find answers for 3) and 4) by saying something overtly unpleasant or inappropriate. "We have a bunch of candidates who are better than you" is one example. For more, see "Dealing with difficult questions" section in Jui (2010).

Looking at brain-teasers from the behavioral angle, it's rather funny how their real purpose is at odds with that originally claimed. A sought-after "independent thinker" who does stuff "outside the box" is unlikely to follow the orders he considers stupid. One cannot have it both ways.

This "stress interviewing" (an official term) would be as good as any other method, except the line separating it from hazing is thin to non-existent. The interviewer is in a perfect position of power with respect to the candidate. The opportunities of having fun at candidate's expense without breaking the law are plenty. Companies don't have to encourage hazing explicitly because, like other types of abuse, it is self-perpetuating. "I kind of went through hell during my brain-teaser interview", a poster from Wilmott.com forum recounts, "now that I'm working here, I ask new candidates the same questions myself. That way, I am restoring a divine balance in the universe".

I even find this poetic. It starts with something like: "You are given nine balls, of which one is defective, and a balance you can use only twice. How do you identify the bad ball?" The candidate solves the puzzle, and, lo and behold, balancing the universe is the next thing on his agenda.

Undoubtedly, being able to deal with abusive people is a valuable skill applicable both on and off The Wall Street. However, when my potential future coworker puts it to the test by hazing me at an interview, it amounts to "destructive testing". When Honda does that by smashing its new model against a concrete wall, it makes sense. With people, it's a bit different. If I manage to go through this "balancing the universe" ordeal with dignity, I will presumably earn my interviewer's respect. Does it not occur to him that, whether I fail or not, I won't have any respect for *him?* Unlike Jiu (2010), I think that the "stressful Wall Street environment calls for some tough interview questions" argument is a lot of dreck. It supplies a pretext for hazing, which is an end in itself.

If you encounter one of those proponents of the universal harmony, I believe the following approach makes sense:

1) When you are asked a weird question, your first reaction will be to ask the opponent why he asked you this. Don't do that. Whether you are bullied or not, asking the interviewer to explain himself has no upside for you. Hide your displeasure and answer the question with calm and dignity.

2) Remember that one of your goals is to gather information about the company, which is not an easy task. Your opponent's inappropriate behavior discloses some important, albeit negative, information about your future work environment. Oddly enough, it can be seen as a favor done to you, a "fair warning" about what lies ahead.

3) Suppose your opponent's goal is to "stress test" you to see how far *you* are willing to go to get the position. Why don't you turn the tables, give him a free hand, and see how far *he* is willing to go with that? If, after the interview is over, you decide that he went too far, you can always quit the interview process and/or reject an extended job offer.

4) If you decide to complain about something you didn't like during an interview, do NOT do it via email. An email can be easily forwarded to anyone, and, before you know it, the entire quant industry will learn that you are not too willing to become a considerate spouse.

*Good luck with your future marriage!*

**9 How do we know that you know C++? Getting certified.**

The article of Joshi (publicly available online) provides a good classification of quant job types. "Quantitative Developer" is a fancy title for a person who develops financial software. It doesn't sound very attractive to a PhD-level job-seeker, who would probably prefer "Quantitative Researcher". However, a DC can't afford to be that picky. Besides, even a quant researcher can be required to do lots of programming. Back in 2008, I went through a number of job postings to find out what software skills were in demand. I deliberately tried to consider only the postings that were not about "hard core" quant development. Based on 143 observations, the results are as follows:

1) C++, 42%
2) Excel VBA, 18%
3) Matlab, 11%
4) Java, 9%
5) S+/R, 8%
6) C#, 4%
7) Perl, 3%

Apparently, C++ is the dominant requirement for quant researchers, and even more so for quant developers.

I am going to assume that you have less than a year of industrial (university coursework doesn't count) C++ experience. In that case, the best way to show that you "know C++" is to get certified on Brainbench, www.brainbench.com , and display the results in your CV. It's a well known benchmark in the U.S., and some banks use it directly to screen candidates: you submit a job application and get a link to a pre-paid online Brainbench test.

As of 10/2010, Brainbench.com offers the following C++ tests:

1) "C++", $50
2) "C++ Practice Test", $25
3) "C++ Fundamentals", $50
4) "CORBA C++", $50
5) "Visual C++", $50

Your target test is 1), "C++", and 2) and 3) can be used for practice. You can choose what test results are (not) shown in your publicly available transcript. If you take a test more than 4 times in a 90-day period, it will be noted in your transcript. If you create an account in advance, you are likely to get some credits by participating in the beta-testing and save money.

The test itself is an online, multiple choice, with 5 possible answers for each of 40 questions. Your target score is 90% or higher, meaning that you should do better than 90% of the people who have taken the test before you. As of 10/2010, the number of such people is about 8300, but it's not as scary as it seems. Since the test focuses on the syntax of C++, having industrial experience is not required. Moreover, experience is a bad thing: the test often exploits "dark corners" of the language that are avoided in practice, and that's why some experienced C++ developers complain that the test is inadequate. However, this is beside the point: the only reasonable application of Brainbench score is to screen the initial pool of *entry-level* candidates. More experienced people are (or, at least, should be) evaluated based on the actual software projects they completed.

I suggest you start by taking a beginner and mid-level C++ courses at your university. In theory, you don't have to do that, but then you won't have had any practical experience at all. Even if you get 99% on Brainbench, I'm not sure how you can sell your "theoretical" C++ skills to an employer. After you get to the intermediate level, proceed as follows:

Step 1) Take "C++ Practice Test" (the results are not shown on your transcript), see what your weak areas are, and brush up on them.

Step 2) Take "C++ Fundamentals". If it's over 85%, continue to Step 3). Otherwise, you need to work more on the fundamentals by going through some mid-level books. There are many good ones, and I'm not providing any references here.

Step 3) Disclosing the "C++" test questions is not allowed, but of course they leak out. You can find some using "C++ Brainbench" as keywords and the following search engines:

www.google.com
http://www.baidu.com/
http://www.yandex.ru/
http://www.guruji.com/

The last three are Chinese, Russian, and Indian engines. Of course, the comments to the questions are not going to be in English, but the questions themselves are copied from Brainbench and pasted elsewhere "as is".

Step 4) To acquire advanced level, get the book of Stroustrup (2000). In that particular book, you have to read chapters: 9, 13, 14, 16-21. I am going to give you a detailed list of topics to cover. That way, if you get another version of Stroustrup, you'll know what to focus on.

1) Source files and external / internal linkage

2) Templates

3) Exceptions. The hierarchy of standard exceptions (draw a separate picture for this).

4) All standard containers (vector, list, map, etc), their data members / member functions.

5) Generic algorithms

6) Function objects

7) Iterators (random access, bidirectional, etc). Conversion from regular to reverse iterator and back. Insert iterators, e.g. front_inserter.

8) Strings, with emphasis on the differences among a "character array", a "C string", and a "C++ string object"

9) Stream classes, their data members / member functions. Hierarchy of stream classes and how it is mapped into the header files, such as <iostream>, <fstream>, etc. I suggest you draw a separate scheme for this.

I didn't do any exercises from Stroustrup, because they are not that helpful for Brainbench. Keep in mind that your current goal is to learn the syntax. Correspondingly, any exercise that tries to develop your programming style is irrelevant. The Brainbench questions you saw in Steps 1-3) are quite representative of what you are going to have in the "C++" test.

Step 5) Read the book of Steve Oualline (2003).

Step 6) Study a few C++ features I illustrate below this list.

Step 7) Get the book of Josuttis (1999). This book is an STL reference, and you can use it for finding answers to some peculiar STL questions.

Step 8) Find the latest version of "C++ ISO/IEC standard" online. Usually, it's a large PDF file that describes the language in dry terms. It doesn't make sense to read it, but you can find answers to some difficult questions there.

Step 9) Find or make (e.g., in Excel) a C++ electronic reference source where you could look up the specifications of standard objects (string, map, exception, etc) and functions. A good online reference is:

http://www.cplusplus.com/reference/

Having an electronic reference at hand is crucial, because, for instance, you will be expected to know every specification of "sort" function that exists in STL. A paper book is not going to work because it takes too much time to look it up.

Step 10) Finally, take "C++" test and learn from your experience. While taking the test, keep the reference and the standard open in separate windows (which is officially allowed by Brainbench). Some people suggest finding answers via Google, but it doesn't work. Likewise, having a C++ compiler open (which is not allowed) won't get you far, because the corresponding code in Brainbench window is likely to be a picture, not text that can be copied and pasted.

Referring to Step 6), there are some Brainbench questions based on the features of C++ that are not well reflected in the sources above. I give a few examples below (the code will look better if you use Kindle PC or Mac).

1) Exceptions of primitive types and some peculiar implicit type conversions. Question: in the code below, what type of exception is thrown and where is it caught? This is a "perfect" Brainbench question where experienced developers are likely to fail because nobody uses that stuff in practice, and the correct answer is not intuitive.

```cpp
#include<iostream>
using namespace std;

int main() {
  char c1 = 'a';
  int k1 = 3;
  double f1 = 3.5;

  try {
    throw (c1 + k1);
  }
  catch(long) {
    cout << "Caught long" << endl;
  }
  catch(const char) {
    cout << "Caught const char" << endl;
  }
  catch(int&) {
    cout << "Caught int" << endl;
  }
  catch(short) {
    cout << "Caught short" << endl;
  }
  catch(...) {
    cout << "Caught ..." << endl;
```

```
    }
}
```

2) Friendship between template functions or objects. Question: given the code below, describe the relationship between:

    a) Function fun1 and class C1

    b) Function fun2 and class C2

    c) Function fun1 and class C3

    d) Function fun2 and class C3

    e) Function fun3 and class C3

```cpp
double fun1(double d) {
   return d * 2;
}

template<class T> class C1 {
   T data1;
   friend double fun1(double);
};

template<class A1, class A2> A2 fun2(A1 arg) {
   return arg ^ 2;
}

template<class K1> K1 fun3(K1 arg) {
   return arg ^ 3 - 2 * arg;
}

class C2 {
   int data2;
   template<class A1, class A2> friend A2 fun2(A1);
};

template<class F1, class F2> class C3 {
   friend double fun1(F1);
   // the line above may cause a warning
   friend F2 fun2<F1, F2>(F1);
   template<class K1> friend K1 fun3(K1);
};
```

3) Partial specialization for template classes and its resolution. Question: given the code below, which template specialization is used for creating objects "a" through "f", correspondingly. Note: one of the lines in main() will cause a compile-time error.

```cpp
#include<iostream>
using namespace std;

template<class T, class U, int I> struct X
{
  void f()
  {
    cout << "Primary template" << endl;
  }
};

template<class T, int I> struct X<T, T*, I>
{
  void f()
  {
    cout << "Partial specialization 1" << endl;
  }
};

template<class T, class U, int I> struct X<T*, U, I>
{
  void f()
  {
    cout << "Partial specialization 2" << endl;
  }
};

template<class T> struct X<int, T*, 10>
{
  void f()
  {
    cout << "Partial specialization 3" << endl;
  }
};

template<class T, class U, int I> struct X<T, U*, I> {
  void f()
```

```cpp
  {
    cout << "Partial specialization 4" << endl;
  }
};

int main()
{
  // to get answers, call .f() on all
  // objects constructed below
  X<int, int, 10> a;
  X<int, int*, 5> b;
  X<int*, float, 10> c;
  X<int, char*, 10> d;
  X<float, int*, 10> e;
  X<int, int*, 10> f;
}
```

4) Traversal of the inheritance graph and the order of object construction. Question: given the code below, what is going to be printed out when object "c1" is constructed in main()?

```cpp
#include<iostream>
using namespace std;

class A {
  public:
  int data1;

  A()
  {
    cout << "No-arg constructor for A" << endl;
  }
  A(int k) : data1(k)
  {
    cout << "Int constructor for A" << endl;
  }
};

class B1 : public A
{
  public:
  B1() {
```

```cpp
      cout << "No-arg constructor for B1" << endl;
   }
};

class B2 : virtual public A
{
  public:
  B2() {
    cout << "No-arg constructor for B2" << endl;
  }
};

class X1
{
  public:
  double datax1;
  X1(double d): datax1(d) {cout << "datax1(d)" << endl;}
  X1() {cout << "No-arg constructor for X1" << endl;}
};

class X2
{
  public:
  double datax2;
  X2(double d): datax2(d) {cout << "datax2(d)" << endl;}
  X2() {cout << "No-arg constructor for X2" << endl;}
};

class X3
{
  public:
  double datax3;
  X3(double d) : datax3(d) {cout << "datax3(d)" << endl;}
  X3() {cout << "No-arg constructor for X3" << endl;}
};

class C : public B1, public B2 {
  public:
  X2 cx2;
  X1 cx1;
  X3 cx3;

  C()
```

```cpp
  {
    cout << "No-arg constructor for C" << endl;
  }
  C(double d1, double d2, double d3) : cx1(X1(d1)), cx2(X2(d2))
  {
    cout << "3-arg constructor for C" << endl;
    cx3 = X3(d3);
  }
};

int main()
{
  C c1(10.2, 15.5, -5.5);
}
```

Needless to say, your prospective employer will re-test you by giving you a Brainbench-like online test and/or during a personal interview. For the in-person interview, the preparation should be different from what you did for Brainbench, because it's not about syntax and multiple choice any more. I believe the most useful preparation source is Joshi (2008B). It demonstrates how the major features of C++ (inheritance and virtual functions, smart pointers, pointers to member functions, etc) can be put to use in the context of quant development. The books of Meyers and Sutter have also received much praise, but they are not related to quantitative finance. In addition, there are lots of online sources, e.g.:

http://www.parashift.com/c++-faq-lite/
Keywords: *C++ FAQ Frequently Asked Questions Marshall Cline*

## 10 Conclusion and online FAQ

I have five years of quant job search experience, and, essentially, I turned myself into a headhunter more qualified than a great many "recruiting professionals" in the field. The point is, I never signed up for this. Like all of you, I'd rather spend my time on quant modeling than on practicing the firmness of my handshake or learning the intricacies of LinkedIn. Alas, I see no way around this: if you are a DC, you must invest substantial time, effort, and money in your job search. No one is going to do it for you, although this guide will save you a lot of trouble.

I am sure you will come up with your own job search solutions as long as you take the message above seriously. The advances of technology will help you out. As I am writing this, LinkedIn website is shut down because it is being upgraded with new features. Drastically new avenues of putting oneself in front of the employer are bound to appear in the near future and make this manual as obsolete as a handwritten resume is today.

Finally, I would like to let you have some means of providing feedback and asking questions. If you have a question about "soft" interviewing, the best option is to ask it through the blog of Marina Byezhanova. Marina is a partner at ProNexia, a headhunting firm based in Montreal, Canada.

www.ingramcontent.com/pod-product-compliance
Lightning Source LLC
Chambersburg PA
CBHW020507160726
47991CB00007B/2837